THEY'VE PUT CUSTARD WITH MY BONE!

THE Footrot Flats SERIES
BY Murray Ball.

Footrot Flats 1
Footrot Flats 2
Footrot Flats 3
Footrot Flats 4
Footrot Flats 5
Footrot Flats 6
Footrot Flats 7
Footrot Flats 8
Footrot Flats 9
They've put custard with my bone!
The cry of the grey ghost
I'm warning you, Horse . . .

THEY'VE PUT CUSTARD WITH MY BONE!

BY
Murray Ball.

ORIN BOOKS

First published in Australia March, 1983.
Reprinted September 1983, April 1985.
World copyright. All rights reserved.
© Murray Ball 1982-83.
Published by Orin Books, P.O. Box 89, St. Kilda West, Victoria, Australia 3182.

Printed by The Dominion Press–Hedges & Bell, Victoria.
ISBN 0 9592263 0 3

Syndicated internationally outside New Zealand by Inter Continental Features, P.O. Box 89, St. Kilda West, Vic. Australia 3182.

FOOTROT FLATS comic strip is now appearing in the Sydney DAILY MIRROR and SUNDAY TELEGRAPH, Melbourne HERALD, Brisbane COURIER MAIL and SUNDAY MAIL, Perth WEST AUSTRALIAN and WEEKEND NEWS, Adelaide NEWS and SUNDAY MAIL, Canberra TIMES and SUNDAY TIMES, Launceston EXAMINER and SUNDAY EXAMINER, and many other newspapers around Australia too numerous to list individually.

The selection of cartoon strips in this book and the individual cartoons in it are fully copyright. Permission must be obtained in writing from the publishers before reproducing any cartoon strip or cartoon by any means.

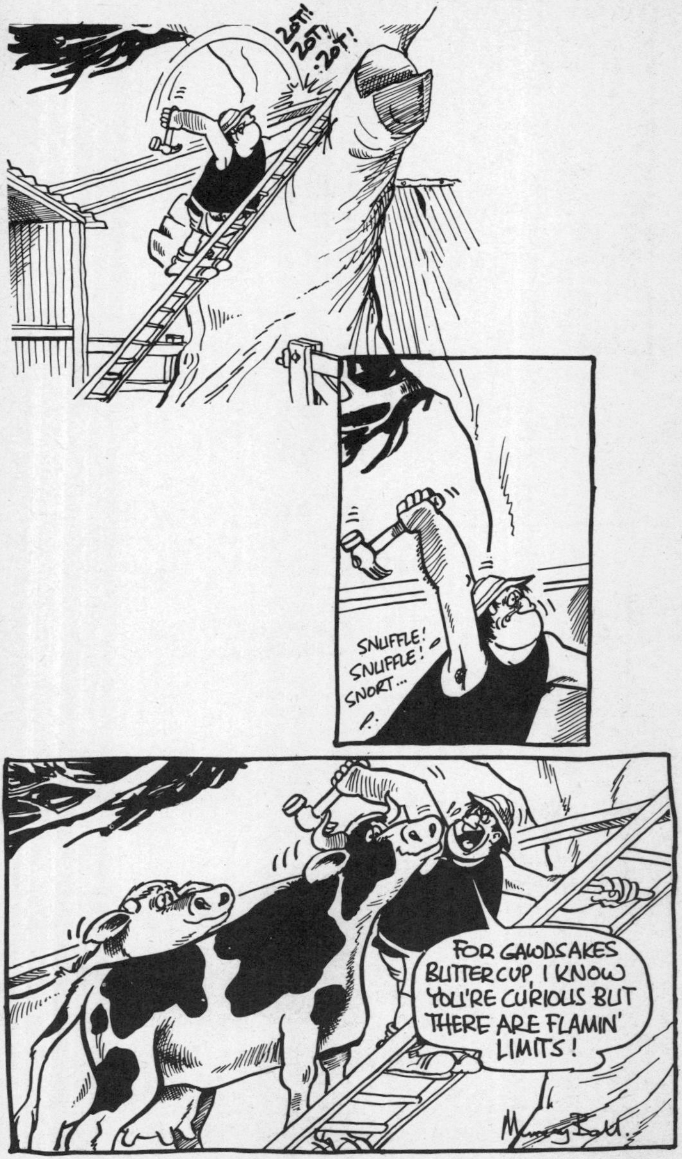

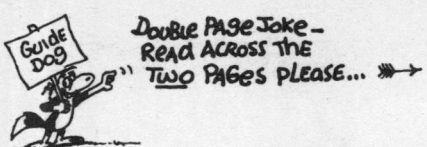

Double page joke – Read across the two pages please... →

1. Look at old Cecil the ram in action! He may be old but you've gotta admire his technique – he's got the ewes eating out of his hoofs!

5. The spirit is willing but the old flesh lets him down a bit at times...

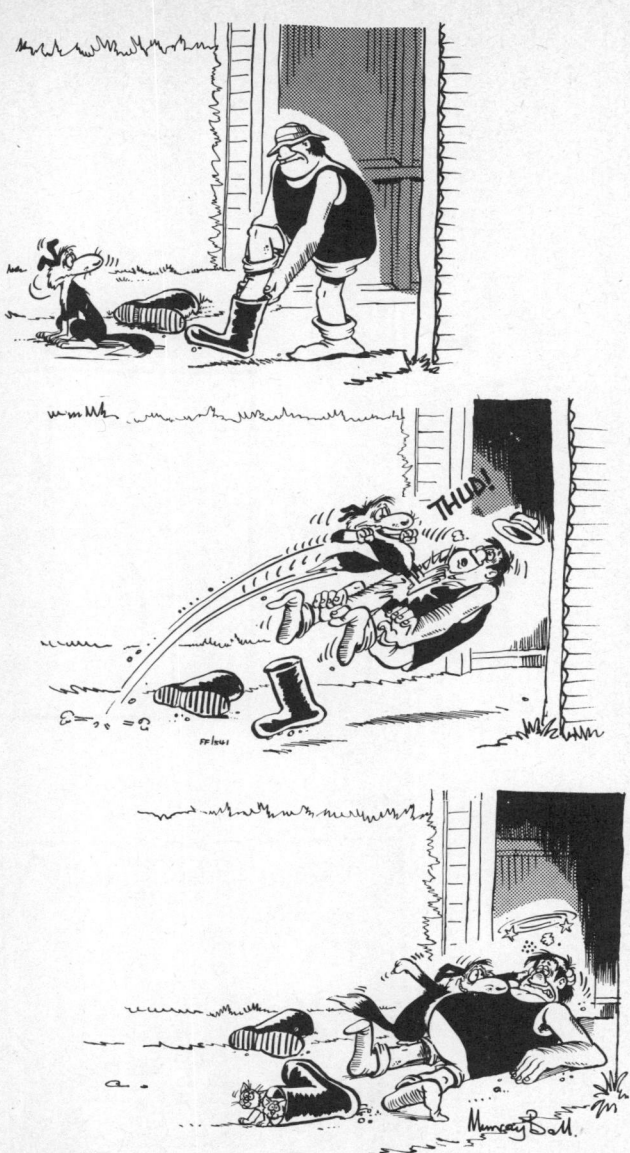

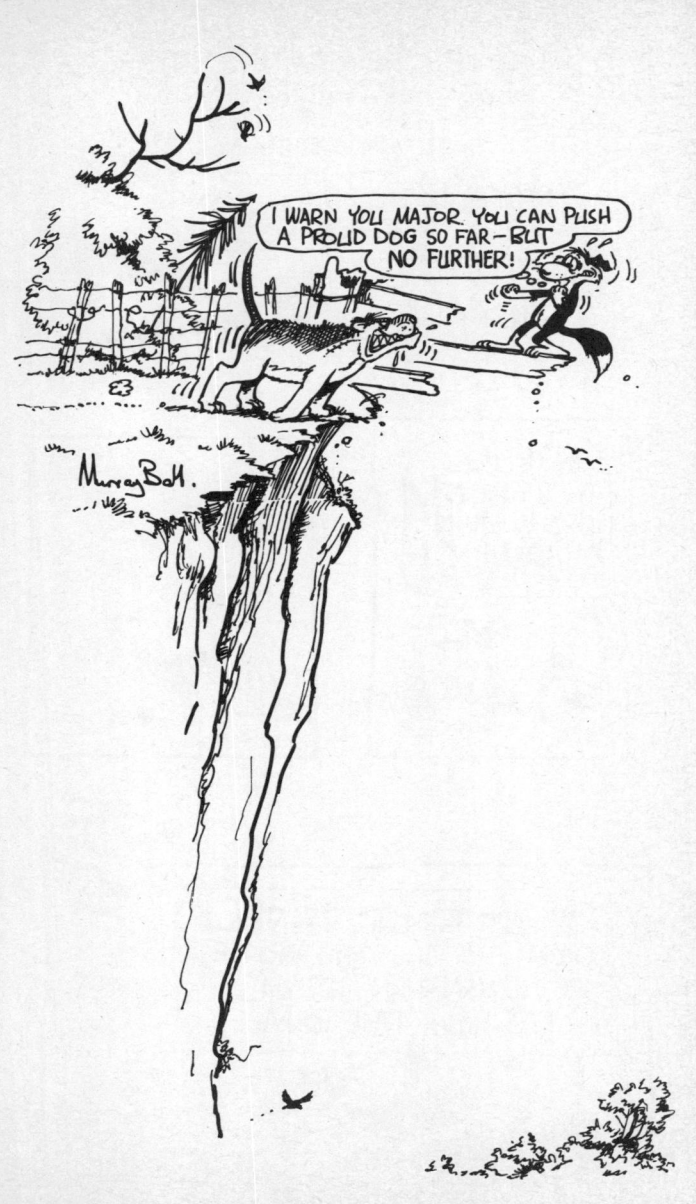

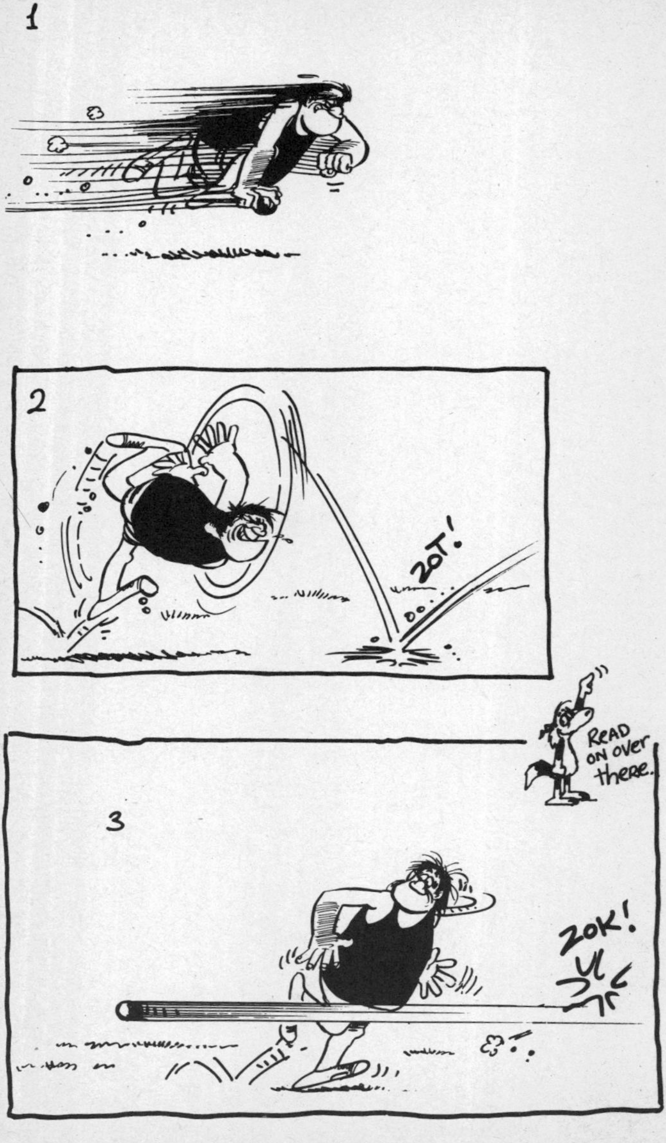

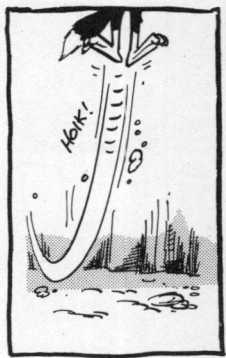

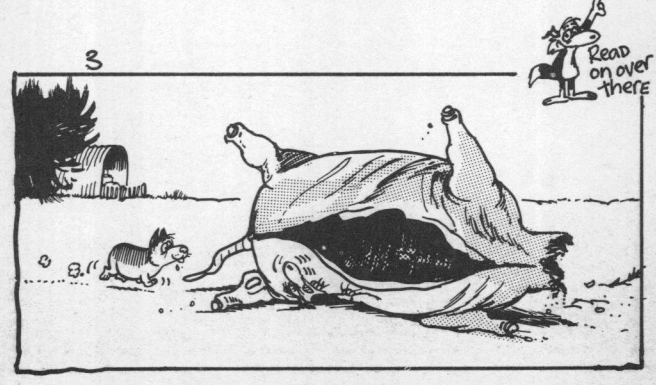

Read on over there

4

5

6